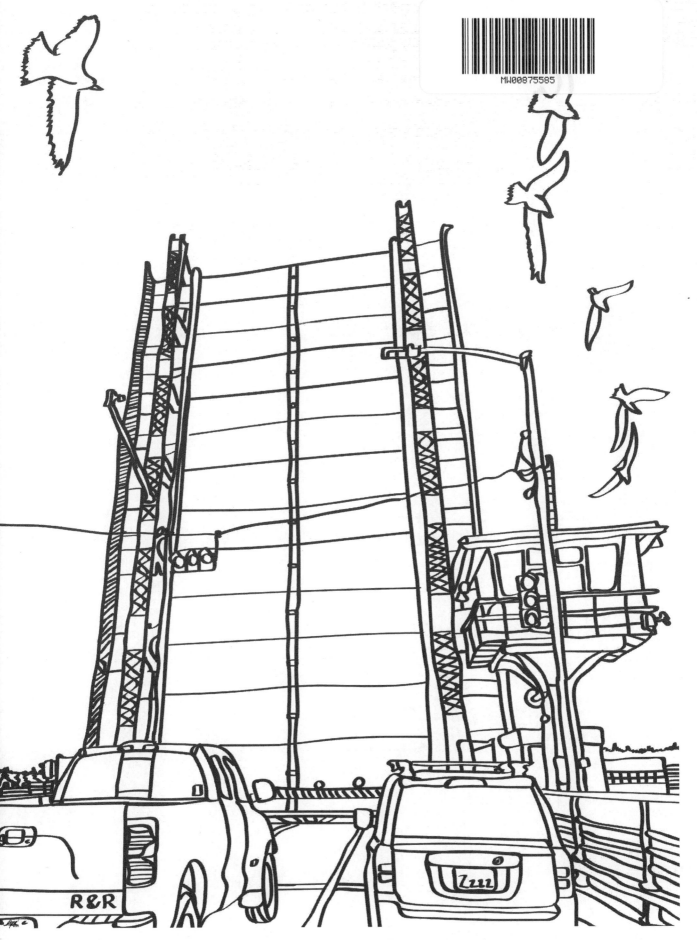

MW00875585

Ballard Bridge

Ballard Locks

Waterfront Carriage

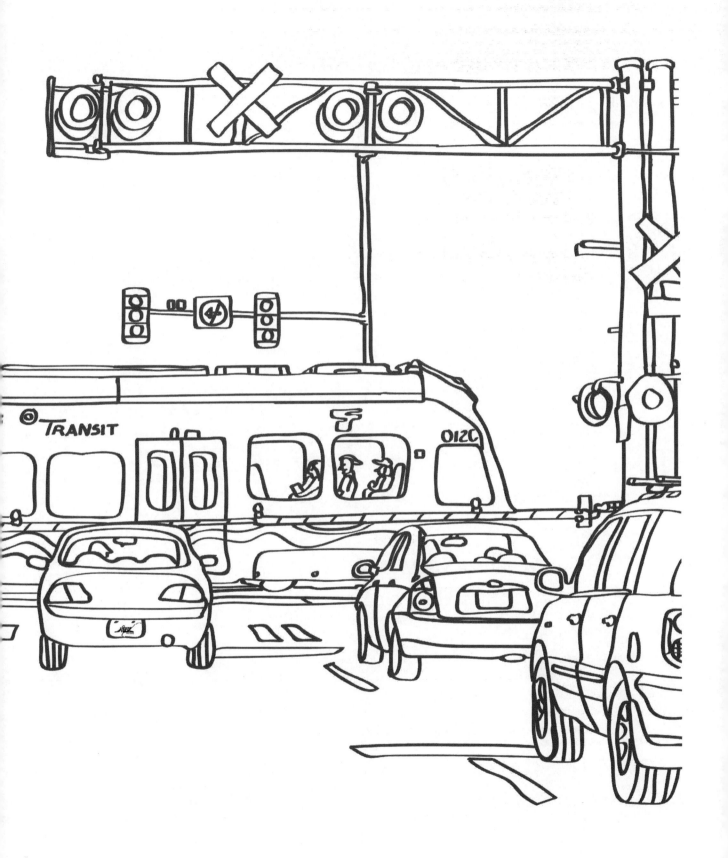

Stopped for Transit

Ballard Crab Boat

King Street Station

DOG PARK
4 AM - 1130 PM

Dog Park

Downtowne Market

Fisherman's Wharf

Market Flowers

Solstice Parade Participants

Heron Observing Greenlake Rowers

ONE
WAY

Public Downtowne Library

Monorail

Traffic Near Mt. Rainier

No Parking

Sasquatch at the Beach

Sunday Afternoon

Streetcar in Seattle

Science Center & Space Needle